PERSONAL FINANCIAL PLANNER

to accompany

PERSONAL FINANCE
Second Edition

Jack R. Kapoor
College of DuPage

Les R. Dlabay
Lake Forest College

Robert J. Hughes
Richland College

Developed by

Les R. Dlabay
Lake Forest College

IRWIN
Homewood, IL 60430
Boston, MA 02116

Printed in the United States of America.

ISBN 0-256-08584-6

1 2 3 4 5 6 7 8 9 0 VK 7 6 5 4 3 2 1 0

PERSONAL FINANCIAL PLANNER

PREFACE

The *Personal Financial Planner* is packaged free of charge with each copy of *Personal Finance*, Second Edition, by Kapoor, Dlabay, and Hughes purchased from Irwin. This resource manual is designed to assist you in creating and implementing your own personal financial plan. The worksheets in this *Personal Financial Planner* are divided into three main sections.

> **SECTION I—Building and Implementing Your Personal Financial Plan** presents the worksheets necessary for assessing your current financial situation and for deciding what actions need to be taken. This is the starting point for your financial planning activities.

> **Section II—Financial Planning Summary** provides sheets that summarize your current financial situation, offers a progress check on financial goals and activities, and suggests actions that need to be taken based on decisions from the sheets in Sections I and III.

> **Section III—Researching Personal Finance Decisions** offers worksheets for evaluating alternative courses of action when considering specific financial decision-making situations.

NOTES BEFORE YOU MOVE FORWARD . . .

- Since this resource manual is designed to adapt to every personal financial situation, some of the documents may be inappropriate for you at this time. Each of the sheets in Sections I and III are referenced to specific page numbers of *Personal Finance*, Second Edition, to help you improve your understanding of the topic.

- Next, some sheets may need to be used more than once (such as those for preparing a personal cash flow statement or a budget). Consider recording your data in pencil so changes can be made, or duplicate the sheets that you may need to use more than once, such as determining life insurance needs for two household members.

- Finally, remember that personal financial planning is an on-going activity. With the use of this resource book and the textbook and your continuing efforts, an organized and satisfying personal economic existence can be yours.

TABLE OF CONTENTS

SECTION I -- PREFACE

Building and Implementing Your Personal Financial Plan

This section of the *Personal Financial Planner* is designed to provide the basic foundation for your financial plan. The worksheets will help you assess your current situation, set goals, and plan for actions to achieve these financial objectives. Suggested actions from this section will be summarized on the sheets in Section II, while Section III provides additional research assistance for certain topics.

--A--
Planning Your Personal Finances

> 1--Personal information sheet
> 2--Financial documents and records
> 3--Personal balance sheet
> 4--Personal cash flow statement
> 5--Goal setting sheet
> 6--Cash budget
> 7--Current income tax estimate
> 8--Tax planning activities

--B--
Managing Your Personal Finances

> 1--Using savings to achieve financial goals
> 2--Consumer credit usage patterns (inventory of debts)

--C--
Making Your Purchasing Decisions

> 1--Comparing cash and credit for major purchases
> 2--Current and future housing needs
> 3--Housing affordability and mortgage qualification
> 4--Current and future transportation needs

--D--
Managing Your Financial Risks

> 1--Current insurance policies and needs
> 2--Determining needed property insurance
> 3--Determining life insurance needs
> 4--Assessing current and needed health care insurance
> 5--Determining life insurance needs

--E--
Investing Your Financial Resources

> 1--Setting investment objectives
> 2--Using stocks to achieve financial goals
> 3--Using bonds to achieve financial goals
> 4--Using mutual funds, and other investments

--F--
Controlling Your Financial Future

> 1--Forecasting retirement income needs
> 2--Estate planning activities
> 3--Estate tax projection and settlement costs

PERSONAL INFORMATION SHEET

- **Purpose** To provide quick reference for vital household data.
- **Instructions** Provide the personal and financial data requested below.

Name _____   _____

Birth Date _____   _____

Marital Status _____   _____

Address _____   _____

_____   _____

Phone _____

Social Security
Number _____   _____

Drivers License No. _____   _____

Place of
employment _____   _____

Address _____   _____

_____   _____

Phone _____   _____

Position _____   _____

Length of Service _____   _____

Checking Account
No. _____   _____

Financial
Institution _____   _____

Address _____   _____

_____   _____

Phone _____   _____

Dependent data:

Name	Birth date	Relationship	Social Security Number
_____	_____	_____	_____
_____	_____	_____	_____
_____	_____	_____	_____
_____	_____	_____	_____
_____	_____	_____	_____

2

FINANCIAL DOCUMENTS AND RECORDS

Section I Sheet A-2
Personal Finance
Second Ed., Kapoor,
Dlabay & Hughes
Pages 66-69

- **Purpose** To develop a logical system for maintaining and storing personal financial documents and records.
- **Instructions** Indicate the location of the following financial records.

Location	Home file	Safe-deposit Box	Other (specify)
Money management records (budget, financial statements)			
Personal/employment records • current resume, social security card			
• educational transcripts			
• birth, marriage, divorce certificates			
• citizenship, military papers			
• adoption, custody papers			
Tax records			
Financial services/consumer credit records • unused, cancelled checks			
• savings, passbooks, statements			
• savings certificates			
• credit card information, statements			
• credit contracts			
Consumer purchase, housing, and automobile records • warranties, receipts			
• owner's manuals			
• lease (if renting) or mortgage papers, title deed, property tax info			
• automobile title			
• auto registration			
• auto service records			
Insurance records • insurance policies			
• home inventory			
• medical information (health history)			
Investment records • broker statements			
• dividend reports			
• stock/bond certificates			
• rare coins, stamps, and other collectibles			
Estate planning and retirement records • copy of will			
• pension, social security information			

PERSONAL BALANCE SHEET

- **Purpose** To determine the current financial position of yourself or household.
- **Instructions** List the current values of the asset categories below; list the amounts owed for various liabilities; subtract total liabilities from total assets to determine net worth.

Section I Sheet A-3
Personal Finance
Second Ed., Kapoor,
Dlabay & Hughes
Pages 69-73

As of _____

ASSETS

Liquid assets
Checking account balance   _____
Savings/money market accounts, funds   _____
Cash value of life insurance   _____
Other: _____   _____
    Total liquid assets   _____

Household assets and possessions
Current market value of home   _____
Market value of automobiles   _____
Furniture   _____
Clothing   _____
Stereo, video, camera equipment   _____
Jewelry   _____
Other: _____   _____
Other: _____   _____
    Total household assets   _____

Investment assets
Savings certificates   _____
Stocks and bonds   _____
Individual retirements accounts   _____
Mutual funds   _____
Other: _____   _____
    Total investment assets   _____

Total Assets   _____

LIABILITIES

Current liabilities
Charge account and credit card balances   _____
Loan balances   _____
Other: _____   _____
Other: _____   _____
    Total current liabilities   _____

Long-term liabilities
Mortgage   _____
Other: _____   _____
    Total long-term liabilities

Total Liabilities   _____

Net worth   _____
(assets minus liabilities)

4

PERSONAL CASH FLOW STATEMENT

Section I Sheet A-4
Personal Finance
Second Ed., Kapoor,
Dlabay & Hughes
Pages 73-77

- **Purpose** To monitor cash inflows and outflows for a month (or three months).
- **Instructions** Maintain records for all inflows and outflows of cash for a one (or three) month period.

For month ended _____ 19___

CASH INFLOWS (Income)

Salary (take-home pay)   _____
Other income:
Other income: _____

                         Total income   _____

CASH OUTFLOWS (Payments)

Fixed Expenses
   Mortgage or rent   _____
   Loan payments   _____
   Insurance   _____
   Other: _____   _____
   Other: _____   _____
     Total fixed outflows   _____

Variable expenses
   Food   _____
   Clothing   _____
   Electricity   _____
   Telephone   _____
   Water   _____
   Transportation   _____
   Personal care   _____
   Medical expenses   _____
   Recreation/entertainment _____
   Gifts   _____
   Donations   _____
   Other: _____   _____
   Other: _____   _____
     Total variable outflows   _____

                    Total outflows   _____

                    Cash Surplus +   _____
                    (or deficit –)

Allocation of surplus
   Emergency fund savings   _____
   Financial goals savings   _____
   Other savings: _____   _____

GOAL SETTING   Current date _____

Section I Sheet A-5
Personal Finance
Second Ed., Kapoor,
Dlabay & Hughes
Pages 18-20; 78-79

- **Purpose** To identify and create a plan of action for personal financial goals.
- **Instructions** Based on personal and household needs and values, identify specific goals that require action.

SHORT-TERM MONETARY GOALS (less than two years)

Description	Amount needed	Months to achieve	Action to be taken	Priority
Example: pay off credit card debt	$850	12	use money from pay raise	high (medium or low)

INTERMEDIATE AND LONG-TERM MONETARY GOALS (more than two years)

Description	Amount needed	Months to achieve	Action to be taken	Priority

NON-MONETARY GOALS

Description	Time Frame	Actions to be taken
Example: Set up file for personal financial records and documents	next 2-3 months	locate all personal and financial records and documents; set up files for various spending, saving, borrowing categories

CASH BUDGET

- **Purpose** To compare projected and actual spending for a one (or three) month period.
- **Instructions** Estimate projected spending based on your cash flow estimate (Sheet II-A-4) and maintain records for actual spending for these same budget categories.

Section I Sheet A-6
Personal Finance
Second Ed., Kapoor,
Dlabay & Hughes
Pages 79-82

	Budgeted Amounts (dollar)	Budgeted Amounts (percent)	Actual Amounts	Variance
Income				
Salary				
Other: _____				
Total income		100%		
Expenses				
Fixed Expenses				
Mortgage or rent				
Property taxes				
Loan payments				
Insurance				
Other: _____				
Total fixed expenses				
Emergency Fund/Savings:				
Emergency fund				
Savings for: _____				
Savings for: _____				
Total savings				
Variable Expenses:				
Food				
Utilities (telephone, heat, electricity, water)				
Clothing				
Automobile expenses and transportation costs				
Personal care				
Medical and health care				
Entertainment/recreation				
Reading/education				
Gifts/donations				
Personal allowances and miscellaneous expenses				
Other: _____				
Other: _____				
Total variable expenses				
Total Expenses		100%		

CURRENT INCOME TAX ESTIMATE

- **Purpose** To estimate your current federal income tax liability.
- **Instructions** Based on last year's tax return, estimates for the current year, and current tax regulations and rates, estimate your current tax liability.

Section I Sheet A-7
Personal Finance
Second Ed., Kapoor,
Dlabay & Hughes
Pages 98-105

Gross income (wages, salary, investment income, and other ordinary income	$_____
Less: Adjustments to Income (see current tax regulations	$–_____
Equals: Adjusted Gross Income (AGI)	$=_____

Less:	**Standard deduction ... or ... Itemized deduction**	
		• medical expenses (exceeding 7.5 percent of AGI) _____
		• state/local income, property taxes _____
		• mortgage, home equity loan interest _____
		• contributions _____
		• casualty and theft losses _____
		• moving expenses _____ job-related, miscellaneous expenses _____
	Amount $–_____	Total $–_____

Less: Personal exemptions	$–_____
Equals: Taxable Income	$=_____
Estimated tax (based on current tax tables or tax schedules)	$_____
Less: Tax credits	$–_____
Plus: Other taxes	$+_____
Equals: Total tax liability	$=_____
Less: Estimated withholding	$–_____
Equals: tax due or (refund)	$=_____

(NOTE: Use Sheet III-A-5 to compare income tax preparation services)

TAX PLANNING ACTIVITIES

- **Purpose** To consider various actions that can prevent tax penalties and that can result in tax savings.
- **Instructions** Consider whether each of the following actions are necessary and appropriate for your tax situation.

Section I Sheet A-8
Personal Finance
Second Ed., Kapoor,
Dlabay & Hughes
Pages 102; 105-119

Filing status/witholding:	Action to be taken (describe)	Not Appropriate (✓)
• Change filing status or exemptions due to changes in life situation		
• Change amount of withholding due to changes in tax situation		
Tax records, documents • Organize home file for ease of maintaining and retrieving tax data		
• Send current mailing address, correct social security number to IRS, place of employment, and other income sources.		
Annual tax activities: • Be certain all needed data and current tax forms are available well before deadline		
• Research uncertain tax areas		
Tax savings actions: • Consider tax-exempt and tax-deferred investments		
• Attempt to delay receipt of income until the next tax year; pay expenses in current tax year		
• Start or increase use of tax-deferred retirement plans		

USING SAVINGS TO ACHIEVE FINANCIAL GOALS

- **Purpose** To monitor savings for use in reaching financial goals.
- **Instructions** Record the requested savings plan information along with the amount of your balance or income on a periodic basis.

Section I Sheet B-1
Personal Finance
Second Ed., Kapoor,
Dlabay & Hughes
Pages 87-88; 139-146

Regular Savings Account
Account No. _____
Financial Institution:
_____
Address _____
_____
Phone _____

Savings goal/Amount needed/Date needed:
_____
Initial deposit: Date_____   Amount $_____
Balance: Date_____   Amount $_____
                  Date_____   Amount $_____
                  Date_____   Amount $_____
                  Date_____   Amount $_____

Certificates of Deposit
Account No. _____
Financial Institution:
_____
Address _____
_____
Phone _____

Savings goal/Amount needed/Date needed:
_____
Initial deposit: Date_____   Amount $_____
Earnings: Date_____   Amount $_____
                  Date_____   Amount $_____
                  Date_____   Amount $_____
                  Date_____   Amount $_____

Money Market Fund/Account
Account No. _____
Financial Institution:
_____
Address _____
_____
Phone _____

Savings goal/Amount needed/Date needed:
_____
Initial deposit: Date_____   Amount $_____
Balance: Date_____   Amount $_____
Balance: Date_____   Amount $_____
Balance: Date_____   Amount $_____
Balance: Date_____   Amount $_____

U.S. Savings Bonds
Purchase location:
_____
_____
Address _____
_____
Phone _____

Savings goal/Amount needed/Date needed:
_____
Purchase date _____   Maturity date _____
Amount $_____   Maturity value $_____

Purchase date _____   Maturity date _____
Amount $_____   Maturity value $_____

Other savings:
Account No. _____
Financial Institution:
_____
Address _____
_____
Phone _____

Savings goal/Amount needed/Date needed:
_____
Initial deposit: Date_____   Amount $_____
Balance: Date_____   Amount $_____
Balance: Date_____   Amount $_____
Balance: Date_____   Amount $_____
Balance: Date_____   Amount $_____

(NOTE: Sheets III-A-4 and III-B-1 may be used to plan amounts needed to save and to compare costs and benefits of different savings programs.)

CONSUMER CREDIT USAGE PATTERNS
(Inventory of Debts)

- **Purpose** To create a record of current consumer debt balances.
- **Instructions** Record account names, numbers, and payments for current consumer debts.

Section I Sheet B-2
Personal Finance
Second Ed., Kapoor,
Dlabay & Hughes
Pages 166-167

Date _____

Automobile, education, personal, and installment loans

Financial Institution	Account Number	Current Balance	Monthly Payment
_____	_____	_____	_____
_____	_____	_____	_____
_____	_____	_____	_____
_____	_____	_____	_____
_____	_____	_____	_____

Charge accounts and credit cards

_____	_____	_____	_____
_____	_____	_____	_____
_____	_____	_____	_____
_____	_____	_____	_____
_____	_____	_____	_____
_____	_____	_____	_____
_____	_____	_____	_____
_____	_____	_____	_____

Other loans (overdraft protection, home equity, life insurance loan

_____	_____	_____	_____
_____	_____	_____	_____
_____	_____	_____	_____
_____	_____	_____	_____

Totals   _____   _____

Debt payment-to-income ratio = $\dfrac{\text{Total monthly payments}}{\text{net (after-tax) income}}$

COMPARING CASH AND CREDIT FOR MAJOR CONSUMER PURCHASES

Section I Sheet C-1
Personal Finance
Second Ed., Kapoor,
Dlabay & Hughes
Pages 194-199; 229-231

- **Purpose** To compare the costs and benefits of using cash and credit.
- **Instructions** When considering a major consumer purchase, provide the information requested below.

Cash price: Item/Description _____

- Selling price $_____

- Sales tax $_____

- Additional charges (delivery, set up, service contract) $_____

- Discounts (employee discounts, senior citizen or student discounts, discount for paying cash) $_____

- Net cost of item $_____ times ____ percent interest that could be earned times ____ years of use to determine opportunity cost $_____

TOTAL FINANCIAL & ECONOMIC COST WHEN PAYING CASH $_____

Credit price:

- Down payment $_____

- Financing: $_____ a payment for ____ months $_____

- Additional financing charges (application fee, credit report credit life insurance) $_____

- Product-related charges (delivery, set-up) $_____

- Discounts that may apply $ –_____

TOTAL FINANCIAL & ECONOMIC COST WHEN USING CREDIT $_____

Other considerations:

- Will cash used for the purchase be needed for other purposes?

- Will this credit purchase result in financial difficulties?

- Do alternatives exist for this purchasing and payment decision?

(NOTE: Use Sheet III-C-1 to compare brands, stores, features, and prices when making a major consumer purchase)

CURRENT AND FUTURE HOUSING NEEDS

- **Purpose** To assess current and future plans for housing.
- **Instructions** Based on current needs and expected needs, complete the information requested below.

Section I Sheet C-2
Personal Finance
Second Ed., Kapoor,
Dlabay & Hughes
Pages 249-260

Current situation: Date _____

Renting	Buying
Location _____	Location _____
Size, description_____	Size, description_____
_____	_____
Major advantages_____	Major advantages_____
Disadvantages_____	Disadvantages_____
_____	_____
Monthly rent $ _____	Mortgage payment $_____
Lease expiration_____	Balance of mortgage $_____
	Current market value $_____

Expected and projected changes in housing needs:

1. _____

2. _____

3. _____

Personal desires and concerns regarding current housing situation:

1. _____

2. _____

Analysis of future housing situation:

A. Description of new housing situation _____

_____

B. Time when this situation is desired _____

C. Financing resources needed _____

D. Available and projected financial resources _____

E. Concerns that must be overcome _____

_____

F. Realistic time when new housing may be achieved _____

(NOTE: Sheets III-C-3 and 4 may be used to evaluate available apartments and to compare renting versus buying of your housing.)

HOUSING AFFORDABILITY AND MORTGAGE QUALIFICATION AMOUNTS

Section I Sheet C-3
Personal Finance
Second Ed., Kapoor,
Dlabay & Hughes
Pages 264-265

- **Purpose** To estimate the amount of affordable mortgage payment, mortgage amount, and home purchase price.
- **Instructions** Enter the amounts and information requested, and perform the required calculations.

Step 1.   Determine your monthly gross income
            (annual income divided by 12). $_____

Step 2.   With a down payment of at least 10 percent,
            lenders use 28 percent of monthly gross
            income as a guideline for TIPI (taxes,
            insurance, principal, and interest), 36
            percent of monthly gross income as a
            guideline for TIPI plus other debt payments
            (enter .28 or .36).   x_____

                                                                      $_____

Step 3.   Subtract other debt payments (such as payments
            on an auto loan), *if applicable*.   −_____

            Subtract estimated monthly costs of property
            taxes and homeowners insurance.   −_____

            AFFORDABLE MONTHLY MORTGAGE PAYMENT $_____

Step 4.   Divide this amount by the monthly mortgage
            payment per $1,000 based on current mortgage
            rates (see Exhibit 9-9, text p. 265) for
            example, a 10 percent, 30-year loan, the
            number would be $8.78.   ÷_____

            Multipled by $1,000.   x____$1,000

            AFFORDABLE MORTGAGE AMOUNT $_____

Step 5.   Divide your affordable mortgage amount by 1 minus
            the fractional portion of your down payment (for
            example, 0.9 for a 10 percent down payment).   ÷_____

            AFFORDABLE HOME PURCHASE PRICE $_____

(Note: The two ratios used by lending institutions (Step 2) and other loan requirements are likely to vary based on a variety of factors, including the type of mortgage, the amount of the down payment, your income level, and current interest rates. If you have other debts, lenders will calculate both ratios and then use the one that allow you greater flexibility in borrowing.)

CURRENT AND FUTURE TRANSPORTATION NEEDS

- **Purpose** To assess current and future transportation..
- **Instructions** Based on current needs and expected needs, complete the information requested below.

Section I Sheet C-4
Personal Finance
Second Ed., Kapoor,
Dlabay & Hughes
Pages 281-284; 295-298

Current situation: Date _____

Vehicle 1	**Vehicle 2**
Year/Make Model_____	Year/Make/Model_____
Mileage_____	Mileage_____
Condition_____	Condition_____
Needed repairs_____	Needed repairs_____
_____	_____
Estimated annual costs:	Estimated annual costs:_____
• gas, oil, repairs $_____	• gas, oil, repairs $_____
• insurance $_____	• insurance $_____
Loan balance (if any) $_____	Loan balance (if any) $_____
Estimated market value $_____	Estimated market value $_____

Expected and projected changes in transportation needs:

1. _____
2. _____
3. _____

Personal desires and concerns regarding current transportation:

1. _____
2. _____

Analysis of future desired transportation situation:

A. Description of new vehicle situation _____

_____

B. Time when this situation is desired _____

C. Financing resources needed _____

D. Available and projected financial resources _____

E. Concerns that must be overcome _____

_____

F. Realistic time when transportation of choice may be achieved _____

(NOTE: Sheets III-C-6, 7, 8 may be used to assess used cars, to measure auto operating costs, and to evaluate auto leasing)

CURRENT INSURANCE POLICIES AND NEEDS

Section I Sheet D-1
Personal Finance
Second Ed., Kapoor,
Dlabay & Hughes
Pages 316; 323-325

- **Purpose** To establish a record of current and needed insurance coverage.
- **Instructions** List current insurance policies and areas where new or additional coverage is needed.

Area of coverage	Current coverage	Needed coverage
Property insurance	Company_____ Policy No. _____ Coverage amounts _____ Deductible _____ Annual premium_____ Agent _____ Address _____ _____ Phone_____	
Automobile insurance	Company_____ Policy No. _____ Coverages_____ Deductible _____ Annual premium_____ Agent _____ Address _____ _____ Phone_____	
Disability income insurance	Company_____ Policy No. _____ Coverage_____ _____ Contact _____ Phone_____	
Health insurance	Company_____ Policy No. _____ Policy provisions _____ _____ Contact _____ Phone_____	
Life insurance	Company_____ Policy No. _____ Type of policy_____ Amount of coverage_____ Cash value _____ Agent/contact_____ Phone_____	

(NOTE: Use Sheets III-D-1, 2, 3 to compare insurance policies for home, auto, and life coverages)

DETERMINING NEEDED PROPERTY INSURANCE

- **Purpose** To determine property insurance needed for a home or apartment.
- **Instructions** Estimate the value and your needs for the categories below.

Section I Sheet D-2
Personal Finance
Second Ed., Kapoor,
Dlabay & Hughes
Pages 341-343

Real property: (this section not applicable to renters)

Current replacement value of home $_____

Times 80 percent coinsurance provision   .80

Equal amount of insurance for full coverage $_____

Personal property:

Estimated value of appliances, furniture, clothing and
   other household items (conduct a household inventory) $_____

Type of coverage for personal property:
   _____ actual cash value, or
   _____ replacement value

Additional coverage for items with limits on standard personal property coverage such as jewelry, firearms, silverware, photographic and electronic equipment

Item	Amount
_____	_____
_____	_____
_____	_____

Personal liability:

Amount of additional personal liability coverage
   desired for possible personal injury claims $_____

Specialized coverages:

If appropriate, investigate flood or earthquake coverage
   which are excluded from home insurance policies. $_____

(NOTE: Sheet III-D-1 may be used to compare companies, coverages, and costs for apartment or home insurance.)

DISABILITY INCOME INSURANCE NEEDS

- **Purpose** To determine financial needs and insurance coverage related to employment disability situations.
- **Instructions** Use the categories below to determine your potential income needs and disability insurance coverage.

Section I Sheet D-3
Personal Finance
Second Ed., Kapoor,
Dlabay & Hughes
Pages 364-368

Monthly expenses:

	Current	When disabled
Mortgage (or rent)	$_____	$_____
Utilities	$_____	$_____
Food	$_____	$_____
Clothing	$_____	$_____
Insurance payments	$_____	$_____
Debt payments (loans, cards, charge accounts	$_____	$_____
Auto/transportation	$_____	$_____
Medical/dental care	$_____	$_____
Education	$_____	$_____
Personal allowances	$_____	$_____
Recreation, entertainment	$_____	$_____
Contributions, donations	$_____	$_____
TOTAL MONTHLY EXPENSES WHEN DISABLED		$_____ (A)

Substitute income:

	Monthly benefit *
Group disability insurance	$_____
Social security	$_____
State disability insurance plan	$_____
Workers' compensation	$_____
Credit disability insurance (in some auto loan or home mortgages)	$_____
Other income (spouse's income, investments)	$_____
TOTAL PROJECTED INCOME WHEN DISABLED	$_____ (B)

If B is less than A, additional disability income insurance should be considered

(*Most disability insurance programs have a waiting period before benefits start, and may have a limit as to how long benefits are received.)

ASSESSING CURRENT AND NEEDED HEALTH CARE INSURANCE

Section I Sheet D-4
Personal Finance
Second Ed., Kapoor,
Dlabay & Hughes
Pages 368-373

- **Purpose** To assess current and needed medical and health care insurance.
- **Instructions** Investigate your existing medical and health insurance coverage, and determine the need for potential additional coverages.

Insurance company _____

Address _____

Type of insurance   _____ individual health policy
                           _____ group health policy

Premium amount $ _____ (monthly/quarter/semi-annual/annual; circle one)

Main coverages _____

_____

Amount of coverage for:

- hospital costs _____

- surgery costs _____

- physicians' fees _____

- lab tests _____

- out-patient expenses _____

- maternity _____

- major medical _____

Other items covered: _____ Amount $_____

                     _____ Amount $_____

Policy restrictions (deductibles, coinsurance, maximum limits) _____

_____

_____

Items not covered by this insurance _____

_____

Of the items not covered, would supplemental coverage be appropriate for your personal situation? _____

_____

What actions related to your current (or proposed additional) coverage are necessary? _____

_____

_____

DETERMINING LIFE INSURANCE NEEDS

- **Purpose** To estimate life insurance coverage to cover expected expenses and future family living costs.
- **Instructions** Estimate the amounts requested for the categories listed.

Section I Sheet D-5
Personal Finance
Second Ed., Kapoor,
Dlabay & Hughes
Pages 391-394

Household expenses to be covered

1. Final expenses (funeral, estate taxes, etc.) $_____

2. Payment of consumer debt amounts $_____

3. Emergency fund $_____

4. College fund $_____

5. Expected living expenses:

- Expected average living expenses $_____

- Expected spouse's average annual income
  after taxes $–_____

- Annual social security benefits $–_____

- Net annual living expenses $_____

- Years until spouse is 90 $_____

- Investment rate factor (see below) $_____

- Total living expenses (net annual living
  expenses times investment rate factor) $_____

6. Total monetary needs $_____

7. Less: Total current investments $–_____

8. Life insurance needs $_____

Investment rate factors

years until spouse is 90	25	30	35	40	45	50	55	60
conservative investment	20	22	25	27	30	31	33	35
aggressive investment	16	17	19	20	21	21	22	23

(NOTE: Use Sheet III-D-3 to compare life insurance policies)

SETTING INVESTMENT OBJECTIVES

Section I Sheet E-1
Personal Finance
Second Ed., Kapoor,
Dlabay & Hughes
Pages 420-423

- **Purpose** To determine specific goals for an investment program.
- **Instructions** Based on short and long term objectives for your investment efforts, enter the items request below.

Description of financial need	Amount	Date Needed	Investment goal (safety, growth, income)	Type of risk (high, medium, low)	Possible investments to achieve this goal

(NOTE: Sheets II-E-2, 3, and 4 may be used to implement specific investment plans to achieve these goals.)

USING STOCKS TO ACHIEVE FINANCIAL GOALS

- **Purpose** To set forth a plan for the investment in stocks to achieve specific financial goals.
- **Instructions** Use current and projected stock values and dividends to create an investment plan for achieving a goal.

Section I Sheet E-2
Personal Finance
Second Ed., Kapoor,
Dlabay & Hughes
Pages 454-457; 459-465

Financial goal/amount	Stock	Value 1	Value 2	Value 3
	Date _____ Company _____ Purchase price per share $_____ Number of shares _____ Total cost including commission $_____	Date _____ Price per share $_____ Total value $_____	Date _____ Price per share $_____ Total value $_____	Date _____ Price per share $_____ Total value $_____
	Date _____ Company _____ Purchase price per share $_____ Number of shares _____ Total cost including commission $_____	Date _____ Price per share $_____ Total value $_____	Date _____ Price per share $_____ Total value $_____	Date _____ Price per share $_____ Total value $_____
	Date _____ Company _____ Purchase price per share $_____ Number of shares _____ Total cost including commission $_____	Date _____ Price per share $_____ Total value $_____	Date _____ Price per share $_____ Total value $_____	Date _____ Price per share $_____ Total value $_____

(NOTE: Different stocks can be used for each financial goal, or a portfolio of several stocks can be used for a single financial goal.)

USING BONDS TO ACHIEVE FINANCIAL GOALS

<table>
<tr><td>
<ul>
<li>Purpose To set forth a plan for the investment in bonds to achieve specific financial goals.</li>
<li>Instructions Use current and projected interest income and bond prices to create an investment plan for achieving a goal.</li>
</ul>
</td>
<td>
Section I Sheet E-3
Personal Finance
Second Ed., Kapoor,
Dlabay & Hughes
Pages 493; 498-499
</td>
</tr>
</table>

Financial goal/amount	Corporate Bonds	Value 1	Value 2	Value 3
	Organization _____ Purchase price $_____ Date _____ Number of bonds ____ Maturity value, date _____ Total cost including commission $_____ Interest rate annual amount ____% $____	Date _____ Price per bond $_____ Total value $_____	Date _____ Price per bond $_____ Total value $_____	Date _____ Price per bond $_____ Total value $_____
		-- Total interest earned to date --		
		_____	_____	_____
	Organization _____ Purchase price $_____ Date _____ Number of bonds ____ Maturity value, date _____ Total cost including commission $_____ Interest rate, annual amount ____% $____	Date _____ Price per bond $_____ Total value $_____	Date _____ Price per bond $_____ Total value $_____	Date _____ Price per bond $_____ Total value $_____
		-- Total interest earned to date --		
		_____	_____	_____
	Organization _____ Purchase price $_____ Date _____ Number of bonds ____ Maturity value, date _____ Total cost including commission $_____ Interest rate, annual amount ____% $____	Date _____ Price per bond $_____ Total value $_____	Date _____ Price per bond $_____ Total value $_____	Date _____ Price per bond $_____ Total value $_____
		-- Total interest earned to date --		
		_____	_____	_____

(NOTE: Different bonds can be used for each financial goal, or a portfolio of several bonds can be used for a single financial goal.)

23

USING MUTUAL FUNDS AND OTHER INVESTMENTS

- **Purpose** To set forth a plan for using mutual funds and other investment vehicles to achieve specific financial goals.
- **Instructions** Use current and projected investment values and incomes to create an investment plan for achieving a financial goal.

Section I Sheet E-4
Personal Finance
Second Ed., Kapoor,
Dlabay & Hughes
Pages 522-523; 529

Financial goal/amount	Mutual Fund	Value 1	Value 2	Value 3
	Company _____ Purchase price $_____ Date ____ Number of shares _____ Total cost including fees $_____ Type of fund: _____	Date _____ NAV (net asset value) Total value $_____	Date _____ NAV (net asset value) Total value $_____	Date _____ NAV (net asset value) Total value $_____
	Company _____ Purchase price $_____ Date ____ Number of shares _____ Total cost including fees $_____ Type of fund: _____	Date _____ NAV (net asset value) Total value $_____	Date _____ NAV (net asset value) Total value $_____	Date _____ NAV (net asset value) Total value $_____
	Other investment (describe): _____ Contact _____ Phone _____ Purchase price $_____ Date _____ Other fees, charges _____	Date _____ Market value $_____ Invest. income $_____	Date _____ Market value $_____ Invest. income $_____	Date _____ Market value $_____ Invest. income $_____

(NOTE: Different investments can be used for each financial goal, or a portfolio of several investments can be used for a single financial goal.)

FORECASTING RETIREMENT INCOME

- **Purpose** To determine the amount needed to save each year to have the necessary funds to cover retirement living costs.
- **Instructions** Estimate the information requested below.

Section I Sheet F-1
Personal Finance
Second Ed., Kapoor,
Dlabay & Hughes
Pages 571-574; 576-590

Estimated annual retirement living expenses:

- Estimated annual living expenses if you retired today $_____

- Future value for _____ years until retirement at expected annual inflation of _____ percent (Use future value of $1, Exhibit 1-5, text page 11 or Exhibit B-1 in Appendix B   X_____

  PROJECTED ANNUAL RETIREMENT LIVING EXPENSES ADJUSTED FOR INFLATION (A) $_____

Estimated annual income at retirement:

- Social security income $_____

- Company pension, personal retirement account income $_____

- Investment and other income $_____

                    TOTAL RETIREMENT INCOME (B) $_____

Additional retirement plan contributions: (If B is less than A)

- Annual shortfall of income after retirement (A-B) $_____

- Expected annual rate of return on invested funds *after* retirement, percentage expressed as a decimal   _____

- Needed investment fund after retirement
  A minus B divided   (C) $_____

- Future value factor of a series of deposits for _____ years until retirement and an expected annual rate of return *before* retirement of _____ percent (Use Exhibit 1-6, text page 11 or Exhibit B-2 in Appendix B)   (D)   _____

- Annual deposit to achieve needed investment fund
  (C divided by D) $_____

ESTATE PLANNING ACTIVITIES

- **Purpose** To develop a plan to handle estate planning and related financial activities.
- **Instructions** Respond to the following questions as a basis for making and implementing an estate plan.

Section I Sheet F-2
Personal Finance
Second Ed., Kapoor,
Dlabay & Hughes
Pages 603-618

Are your financial records, including recent tax forms, insurance policies, and investment and housing documents, organized and easily accessible?	
Do you have a safe-deposit box? Where is it located? Where is the key?	
Location of life insurance policies. Name and address of insurance company and agent.	
Is your will current? Location of copies of your will. Name and address of your lawyer.	
Name and address of your executor.	
Do you have a listing of the current value of assets owned and liabilities outstanding?	
Have any funeral and burial arrangements been made?	
Have you created any trusts? Name and location of financial institution.	
Do you have current information on gift and estate taxes?	
Have you prepared a letter of last instructions? Where is it located?	

ESTATE TAX PROJECTION AND SETTLEMENT COSTS

Section I Sheet F-3
Personal Finance
Second Ed., Kapoor,
Dlabay & Hughes
Pages 618-623

- **Purpose** To estimate the estate tax based on your current financial situation.
- **Instructions** Enter the data requested below to calculate the tax based on current tax rates.

1. **Gross estate values:**

   personal property $_____

   real estate $_____

   joint ownership $_____

   business interests $_____

   life insurance $_____

   employee benefits $_____

   controlled gifts/trusts $_____

   prior taxable gifts $_____

        Total estate values $_____

2. **Deductible debts, costs, expenses:**

   mortgages and secured loans $_____

   unsecured notes and loans $_____

   bills and accounts payable $_____

   funeral and medical expenses $_____

   probate administration costs $_____

        Total deductions $-_____

3. **Charitable bequests** $-_____

4. **Marital deduction** $-_____

5. **Taxable estate** $=_____

6. **Gross estate tax** $_____

7. **Allowable credits**

   Unified credit $_____

   Gift tax credit $_____

   State tax credit $_____

   Foreign tax credit $_____

   Prior tax credit $_____

        Total tax credits $-_____

5. **Net estate tax** $=_____

NOTE: Consult the Internal Revenue Service for current rates and regulations related to estate taxes.

SECTION II -- PREFACE

FINANCIAL PLANNING SUMMARY

This section of the *Personal Financial Planner* is designed to summarize the actions needed to be taken in an effort to assess, plan, and achieve your personal financial goals. The sheets in this section provide an overview of the planning and research activities from Sections I and III.

This section includes the following forms:

- Financial Data/Savings and Investment Portfolio Summary
- Progress Check on Major Financial Goals and Activities
- Summary Sheets for Suggested Actions for:
    A--Planning Your Personal Finances
    B--Managing Your Personal Finances
    C--Making Your Purchasing Decisions
    D--Managing Your Financial Risks
    E--Investing Your Financial Resources
    F--Controlling Your Financial Future

As you complete the various sheets in Section I, transfer actions that need to be taken and the financial data summary to the sheets in this section. For example:

Sheet	Actions to be taken	Planned Completion date	Completed (✓)
I-A-2 Financial Documents and Records	*locate and organize all personal financial documents*	*within 2-3 months*	
I-A-7 Current income tax estimate	*sort current tax data, compute estimate to determine tax amount*	*February 15*	(✓)
I-B-2 Consumer credit usage patterns	*pay off high interest credit cards and charge accounts*	*next 6-12 months*	
I-D-1 Current insurance needs and policies	*locate and list company policy, coverage, and agent information*	*January 15*	(✓)
	obtain additional auto liability coverage	*Immediately*	(✓)

By following this procedure, Section II will provide a condensed summary of needed and completed actions, while Section I will offer supporting details related to these financial planning activities.

FINANCIAL DATA SUMMARY

		Date ___	Date ___	Date ___	Date ___	Date ___
Balance Sheet Summary (Sheet I-A-3)	Assets					
	Liabilities					
	Net Worth					
Cash Flow Summary (Sheet I-A-4)	Inflows					
	Outflows					
	Surplus + (Deficit -)					
Budget Summary (Sheet I-A-6)	Budget					
	Actual					
	Variance (+ / -)					

SAVINGS/INVESTMENT PORTFOLIO SUMMARY

Description	Organization Contact; Phone	Purchase Price; Date	Value; Date	Value; Date	Value; Date
		$_____ _____	$_____ _____	$_____ _____	$_____ _____
		$_____ _____	$_____ _____	$_____ _____	$_____ _____
		$_____ _____	$_____ _____	$_____ _____	$_____ _____
		$_____ _____	$_____ _____	$_____ _____	$_____ _____
		$_____ _____	$_____ _____	$_____ _____	$_____ _____
		$_____ _____	$_____ _____	$_____ _____	$_____ _____
		$_____ _____	$_____ _____	$_____ _____	$_____ _____
		$_____ _____	$_____ _____	$_____ _____	$_____ _____

PROGRESS CHECK ON MAJOR FINANCIAL GOALS AND ACTIVITIES

Some financial planning activities require a short-term perspective such as organizing a home file for financial records or paying off a small loan within the next few months. Other actions may require continued efforts over a long period of time such as purchasing a vacation home or saving for a child's education. This sheet is designed to help you monitor these long-term, ongoing financial activities.

Major financial objective	Desired completion date	Initial actions & date	--- Progress Checks --- (Record date, progress made, and additional actions to be taken)

(NOTE: Entries on this form may come from any of the other worksheets in the *Personal Financial Planner*, especially helpful would be the "Suggested Action Summary Sheets" on the next six pages and Sheet I-A-5 "Goal Setting Sheet.")

FINANCIAL PLANNING SUMMARY SHEET A--
Actions for Planning Your Personal Finances

Sheet	Actions to be taken	Planned Completion date	Completed (✓)
I-A-1 Personal information sheet (p. 2)			
I-A-2 Financial Documents and Records (p. 3)			
I-A-3 Personal Balance Sheet (p. 4)			
I-A-4 Personal cash flow statement (p. 5)			
I-A-5 Goal setting sheet (p. 6)			
I-A-6 Cash budget (p. 7)			
I-A-7 Current income tax estimate (p. 8)			
I-A-8 Tax planning activities (p. 9)			

Any actions required from the research sheets in Section III may be noted in the following areas:

FINANCIAL PLANNING SUMMARY SHEET B--
Actions for Managing Your Personal Finances

Sheet	Actions to be taken	Planned Completion date	Completed (✓)
I-B-2 Using savings to achieve financial goals (p. 10)			
I-B-2 Consumer credit usage patterns (p. 11)			

Any actions required from the research sheets in Section III may be noted in the following areas:

FINANCIAL PLANNING SUMMARY SHEET C--
Actions for Managing Your Purchasing Decisions

Sheet	Actions to be taken	Planned Completion date	Completed (✓)
I-C-1 Comparing cash and credit for major purchases (p. 12)			
I-C-2 Current and future housing needs (p. 13)			
I-C-3 Housing affordability and mortgage qualification (p. 14)			
II-C-4 Current and future transportation needs (p. 15)			

Any actions required from the research sheets in Section III may be noted in the following areas:

FINANCIAL PLANNING SUMMARY SHEET D--
Actions for Managing Your Financial Risks

Sheet	Actions to be taken	Planned Completion date	Completed (✓)
I-D-1 Current insurance policies and needs (p. 16)			
I-D-2 Determining needed property insurance (p. 17)			
I-D-3 Disability income insurance needs (p. 18)			
I-D-4 Assessing current and needed health care insurance (p. 19)			
I-D-5 Determining life insurance needs (p. 20)			

Any actions required from the research sheets in Section III may be noted in the following areas:

FINANCIAL PLANNING SUMMARY SHEET E--
Actions for Investing Your Financial Resources

Sheet	Actions to be taken	Planned Completion date	Completed (✓)
I-E-1 Setting investment objectives (p. 21)			
I-E-2 Using stocks to achieve financial goals (p. 22)			
I-E-3 Using bonds to achieve financial goals (p. 23)			
I-E-4 Using mutual funds and other investment (p. 24)			

Any actions required from the research sheets in Section III may be noted in the following areas:

FINANCIAL PLANNING SUMMARY SHEET F--
Actions for Controlling Your Financial Future

Sheet	Actions to be taken	Planned Completion date	Completed (✓)
I-F-1 Forecasting retirement income needs (p. 25)			
I-F-2 Estate planning activities (p. 26)			
I-F-3 Estate tax projection and settlement costs (p. 27)			

Any actions required from the research sheets in Section III may be noted in the following areas:

SECTION III -- PREFACE

RESEARCHING PERSONAL FINANCE DECISIONS

The worksheets in this section of the *Personal Financial Planner* are designed to assist you when gathering specific data related to various financial decisions. These sheets may be used in conjunction with certain topics in Section II, or may be used to research a specific decision you have under consideration.

--A--
Planning
Your
Personal
Finances

> 1--Resume worksheet
> 2--Career area research sheet
> 3--Employee benefits comparison
> 4--Time value of money calculations
> 5--Income tax preparer comparison

--B--
Managing
Your
Personal
Finances

> 1--Saving plan comparison
> 2--Checking account comparison
> 3--Checking account reconciliation
> 4--Credit card/charge account comparison
> 5--Consumer loan comparison

--C--
Making
Your
Purchasing
Decisions

> 1--Major consumer purchase comparison
> 2--Unit pricing worksheet
> 3--Apartment rental comparison
> 4--Renting vs. buying of housing
> 5--Mortgage company comparison
> 6--Used car purchase comparison
> 7--Automobile ownership and operation costs
> 8--Buying vs. leasing an automobile

--D--
Managing
Your
Financial
Risks

> 1--Apartment/home insurance comparison
> 2--Automobile insurance cost comparison
> 3--Life insurance policy comparison

--E--
Investing
Your
Financial
Resources

> 1--Assessing risk for investments
> 2--Investment broker comparison

--F--
Controlling
Your
Financial
Future

> 1--IRA comparison
> 2--Retirement housing and lifestyle planning

RESUME WORKSHEET

Section III Sheet A-1
Personal Finance
Second Ed., Kapoor,
Dlabay & Hughes
Pages 45-47

- **Purpose** To inventory your education, training, work background, and other experiences for use when preparing a resume.
- **Instructions** List dates, organizations, and other data for each of the categories given below.

Education:

Degree/programs completed	School/location	Dates

Work experience:

Title	Organization/location	Dates	Responsibilities

Other experience:

Title	Organization/location	Dates	Responsibilities

Campus/community activities:

Organization/Location	Dates	Involvement

Honors/Awards:

Title	Organization/Location	Dates

References:

Name	Title	Organization	Address	Phone

CAREER AREA RESEARCH SHEET

Section III Sheet A-2
Personal Finance
Second Ed., Kapoor,
Dlabay & Hughes
Pages 37-41; 42-44

- **Purpose** To become familiar with nature of work and career requirements for a field of employment.
- **Instructions** Using the *Occupational Outlook Handbook* and other career information sources (library materials, interviews), obtain information related to one or more career areas of interest to you.

Career area/job title		
Nature of the work— general activities and duties		
Working conditions— physical surroundings, hours, mental and physical demands		
Training and other qualifications		
Job outlook— future prospect for employment in this field		
Earnings— starting and advanced		
Additional information		
Other questions that require further research		
*Sources of additional information—*publications, trade associations, professional organizations, government agencies		

EMPLOYEE BENEFITS COMPARISON

- **Purpose** To assess the financial and personal value of employment benefits.
- **Instructions** When considering different employment situations, or when selecting benefits within an organization, consider the factors listed below.

Section III Sheet A-3
Personal Finance
Second Ed., Kapoor,
Dlabay & Hughes
Pages 50-54

Organization		
Location		
Phone		
Contact, title		
Health insurance: Company/coverage Cost to be paid by employee		
Disability income insurance: Company/coverage Cost to be paid by employee		
Life insurance: Company/coverage Cost to be paid by employee		
Pension/retirement: Employer contributions Vesting period Tax benefits Employee contributions		
Other benefits/estimated market value: • vacation time • tuition reimbursement • child/dependent care • (other) _____ • (other) _____	$_____ $_____ $_____ $_____ $_____	$_____ $_____ $_____ $_____ $_____

··

TIME VALUE OF MONEY CALCULATIONS

Section III Sheet A-4
Personal Finance
Second Ed., Kapoor,
Dlabay & Hughes
Pages 8-12; 87-88

- **Purpose** To calculate future and present value amounts related to financial planning decisions.
- **Instructions** Use a calculator or future or present value tables to compute the time value of money.

Future value of a single amount:

- to determine future value of a single amount
- to determine interest lost when cash purchase is made

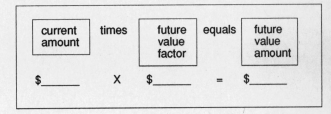

(Use Exhibit 1-5, text page 11, or Exhibit B-1 in Appendix B)

Future value of a series of deposits:

- to determine future values of regular savings deposits
- to determine future value of regular retirement deposits

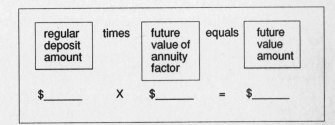

(Use Exhibit 1-6, text page 11, or Exhibit B-2 in Appendix B)

Present value of a single amount:

- to determine an amount to be deposited now that will grow to desired amount

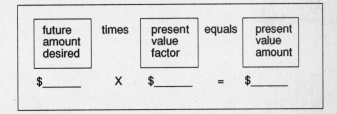

(Use Exhibit 1-7, text page 12, or Exhibit B-3 in Appendix B)

Present value of a series of deposits:

- to determine an amount that can be withdrawn on a regular basis

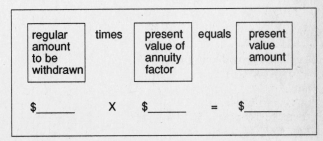

(Use Exhibit 1-8, text page 12, or Exhibit B-4 in Appendix B)

INCOME TAX PREPARER COMPARISON

- **Purpose** To compare the services and costs of different income tax return preparation sources.
- **Instructions** Using advertisements and information from tax preparation services, obtain information for the following.

Section III Sheet A-5
Personal Finance
Second Ed., Kapoor,
Dlabay & Hughes
Pages 113-114

	Local tax service	National tax service	Local accountant
Company name			
Address			
Telephone			
Cost of preparation of Form 1040EZ			
Cost of preparation of Form 1040A			
Cost of preparation of Form 1040 with Schedule 4 (itemized deductions)			
Cost of preparation of state or local tax return			
Assistance provided if IRS questions your return			
Other services provided			

SAVINGS PLAN COMPARISON

Section III Sheet B-1
Personal Finance
Second Ed., Kapoor,
Dlabay & Hughes
Pages 143-146

- **Purpose** To compare the benefits and costs associated with different savings plans.
- **Instructions** Analyze advertisements and contact various financial institutions to obtain the information requested below.

Type of savings plan (regular passbook account, special accounts, savings certificate, money market account, other)			
Financial institution			
Address			
Annual interest rate			
Effective yield			
Frequency of compounding			
Interest method —day of deposit, day of withdrawal —average daily balance —low balance —other _____			
Insured by FDIC, FSLIC, NCUA			
Maximum amount insured			
Minimum initial deposit			
Minimum time period savings must be on deposit			
Penalties for early withdrawal			
Service charges/fees: —transaction fee for more than set number of withdrawals			
—other costs/fees _____			
"Free" gifts —Item —Amount of deposit —Interest lost			

CHECKING ACCOUNT COMPARISON

- **Purpose** To compare the benefits and costs associated with different checking accounts.
- **Instructions** Analyze advertisements and contact various financial institutions (banks, savings and loan associations, or credit unions) to obtain the information requested below.

Section III Sheet B-2
Personal Finance
Second Ed., Kapoor,
Dlabay & Hughes
Pages 147-149

Institution Name			
Address			
Phone			
Type of account (regular checking, NOW account, share drafts, or other)			
Minimum balance for "free" account			
Monthly service charge if minimum balance is not maintained			
Are "free" checking accounts available to full-time students?			
Other checking accounts available and their charges			
Other fees/costs: —printing of checks			
—stop payment order			
—overdrawn account			
—certified check			
—ATM, other charges _____			
Banking hours			
Location of branch offices and ATM terminals			

CHECKING ACCOUNT RECONCILIATION

Section III Sheet B-3
Personal Finance
Second Ed., Kapoor,
Dlabay & Hughes
Pages 151-152

- **Purpose** To determine the adjusted cash balance for your checking account.
- **Instructions** Enter data from your bank statement and checkbook for the amounts requested.

Date of bank statement _____   Account No. _____

BALANCE ON BANK STATEMENT $_____

Step 1:   Subtract total of outstanding checks
(checks that you have written but that have
not yet cleared the banking system)

Check No.	Amount	Check No.	Amount
_____	_____	_____	_____
_____	_____	_____	_____
_____	_____	_____	_____
_____	_____	_____	_____
_____	_____	_____	_____

$–_____

Step 2:   Add deposits in transit
(deposits you have made but that have not been
reported on this statement)

Date	Amount	Date	Amount
_____	_____	_____	_____
_____	_____	_____	_____

$+_____

Adjusted cash balance $_____

CURRENT BALANCE IN YOUR CHECKBOOK $_____

Step 3:   Subtract fees or other charges listed on
your bank statement

Item	Amount	Item	Amount
_____	_____	_____	_____
_____	_____	_____	_____

$–_____

Step 4:   Add interest earned $+_____

Adjusted cash balance $_____

The two adjusted cash balances should be the same; if not, carefully check your math and check to see that deposits and checks recorded in your checkbook and on your bank statement are for the correct amounts.

CREDIT CARD/CHARGE ACCOUNT COMPARISON

Section III Sheet B-4
Personal Finance
Second Ed., Kapoor,
Dlabay & Hughes
Pages 164-166; 200

- **Purpose** To compare the benefits and costs associated with different credit cards and charge accounts.
- **Instructions** Analyze advertisements, credit applications, and contact various financial institutions (banks, savings and loan associations, or credit unions) to obtain the information requested below.

Type of Credit/ Charge Account			
Name of company/account			
Address			
Type of purchases which can be made			
Annual fee (if any)			
Annual percentage rate (APR) information —calculation method used			
Credit limit for new customers			
Minimum monthly payment			
Other costs: —credit report —late fee —other _____			
Restrictions (age, minimum annual income)			
Other information for consumers to consider			

CONSUMER LOAN COMPARISON

- **Purpose** To compare the costs associated with different sources of consumer loans.
- **Instructions** Contact or visit a bank, credit union, and consumer finance company to obtain information on a loan for some specific purpose.

Section III Sheet B-5
Personal Finance
Second Ed., Kapoor,
Dlabay & Hughes
Pages 163-164; 194-196

Purpose of Loan _____ Amount of loan $_____

Type of Financial Institution			
Name			
Address			
Phone			
Amount of down payment			
Length of loan (36 or 48 months, or other _____)			
What collateral is required?			
Amount of monthly payment			
Total amount to be repaid (monthly amount x number of months + down payment)			
Total finance charge/cost of credit			
Annual percentage rate (APR %)			
Other costs: —credit life insurance			
—credit report			
—other costs _____			
Is a co-signer required for the loan?			
Other information			

MAJOR CONSUMER PURCHASE COMPARISON

Section III Sheet C-1
Personal Finance
Second Ed., Kapoor,
Dlabay & Hughes
Pages 225-231

- **Purpose** To research and evaluate brands and store services for purchase of a major consumer item.
- **Instructions** When considering the purchase of a major consumer item, use advertisements, catalogs, store visits, and other sources to obtain the information requested below.

A. Product _____

Exact description (size, model, features, etc.) _____

_____

B. Research the item in consumer periodicals with information regarding your product.

1) article _____ periodical _____

   date _____ pages _____

2) article _____ periodical _____

   date _____ pages _____

C. 1) What buying suggestions are presented in the articles?

2) Which brands are recommended in these articles? Why are they recommended?

D. Contact or visit two or three stores that sell the product to obtain the following information.

	Store 1	Store 2	Store 3
Store name Address			
Phone			
Brand name/cost			
Product differences from item listed above			
Guarantee/warranty offered (describe)			

E. Which brand and at which store would you buy this product? Why?

UNIT PRICING WORKSHEET

Section III Sheet C-2
Personal Finance
Second Ed., Kapoor,
Dlabay & Hughes
Page 234

- **Purpose** To calculate the unit price for a specific consumer purchase.
- **Instructions** Use advertisements or information obtained during store visits to calculate and compare unit prices.

Item (product or service) _____

Date	Store/Location	Brand	Total Price	Size	Unit Price (Total price ÷ Size)	Unit of Measurement (ounce, gallon, etc.)
_____	_____	_____	_____	_____	_____	_____
_____	_____	_____	_____	_____	_____	_____
_____	_____	_____	_____	_____	_____	_____
_____	_____	_____	_____	_____	_____	_____
_____	_____	_____	_____	_____	_____	_____

Highest unit price _____ Store _____ Date _____

Lowest unit price _____ Store _____ Date _____

Difference _____ Store _____ Date _____

Wisest consumer buy: _____ Store _____

Reasons _____

_____

51

··

APARTMENT RENTAL COMPARISON

- **Purpose** To systematically evaluate and compare potential rental housing.
- **Instructions** When in the market for an apartment, obtain information to compare costs and facilities of three apartments.

Section III Sheet C-3
Personal Finance
Second Ed., Kapoor,
Dlabay & Hughes
Pages 253-256

Apartment size: _____ bedroom _____ bath _____ square feet

	A	B	C
Name of renting person or apartment building			
Address			
Phone			
Monthly rent			
Amount of security deposit			
Length of lease			
Utilities included in rent			
Parking facilities (inside/outside)			
Storage area in building			
Laundry facilities available			
Distance to schools (elementary, high school)			
Distance to public transportation (bus, train)			
Distance to shopping			
Pool, recreation area, other facilities			
Type of neighborhood			
Estimated additional costs: Electric			
Telephone			
Gas			
Water			
Other			

RENTING VS. BUYING OF HOUSING

Section III Sheet C-4
Personal Finance
Second Ed., Kapoor,
Dlabay & Hughes
Pages 250-252

- **Purpose** To compare cost of renting and buying your place of residence.
- **Instructions** Obtain estimates for comparable housing units for the data requested below.

RENTAL COSTS

- Annual rent payments $_____

- Renter's insurance $_____

- Interest lost on security deposit (security deposit times after-tax savings account interest rate) $_____

                        TOTAL ANNUAL COST OF RENTING $_____

BUYING COSTS

- Annual mortgage payments $_____

- Property taxes (annual costs) $_____

- Homeowner's insurance (annual premium) $_____

- Estimated maintenance and repairs (____ percent of home value) $_____

- After-tax interest lost because of down payment and closing costs $_____

Less: (financial benefits of home ownership)

- Growth in equity $-_____

- Tax savings for mortgage interest (annual mortgage interest times tax rate) $-_____

- Tax savings for property taxes (annual property taxes times tax rate) $-_____

- Estimated annual depreciation (____ percent) $-_____

                        TOTAL ANNUAL COST OF BUYING $_____

MORTGAGE COMPANY COMPARISON

Section III Sheet C-5
Personal Finance
Second Ed., Kapoor,
Dlabay & Hughes
Pages 264-272

- **Purpose** To compare the services and costs for different sources of home mortgages.
- **Instructions** When in the process of obtaining a mortgage, obtain the information requested below from different mortgage companies.

Amount of mortgage $_____   Down payment $_____   ____ years

Company			
Address			
Phone			
Contact person			
Application, credit report, property appraisal fees			
Loan origination fee			
Other fees, charges (commitment, title, tax transfer)			
Fixed rate mortgage			
Monthly payment			
Discount points			
Adjustable rate mortgage --time until first rate change --frequency of rate change			
Monthly payment			
Discount points			
Payment cap			
Interest rate cap			
Rate index used			
Commitment period			

USED CAR PURCHASE COMPARISON

- **Purpose** To research and evaluate different types and sources of used cars.
- **Instructions** When considering a used car purchase, use advertisements and visits to new and used car dealers to obtain the information requested below.

Section III Sheet C-6
Personal Finance
Second Ed., Kapoor,
Dlabay & Hughes
Pages 285-288

	Private Party	Used Car Dealer	New Car Dealer
Automobile (year, make, model)			
Name			
Address			
Phone			
Cost			
Mileage			
Condition of auto			
Condition of tires			
Radio			
Air Conditioning			
Other options			
Warranty (describe, if any)			
Items in need of repair			
Inspection items: any rust?			
worn shock absorbers?			
oil or fluid leaks?			

AUTOMOBILE OWNERSHIP AND OPERATION COSTS

- **Purpose** To calculate or estimate the cost of owning and operating an automobile or other vehicle.
- **Instructions** Maintain records related to the cost categories listed below.

Section III Sheet C-7
Personal Finance
Second Ed., Kapoor,
Dlabay & Hughes
Pages 295-298

Model year _____ Make, size, model _____

FIXED OWNERSHIP COSTS

1.	Depreciation	Purchase price $_____ divided by estimated life of _____ years (*)	$_____
2.	Interest on auto loan	Annual cost of financing vehicle if buying on credit	$_____
3.	Insurance for the vehicle	Annual cost of liability and property	$_____
4.	License, registration fee, and taxes	Cost of registering vehicle for state and city license fees	$_____
	TOTAL FIXED COSTS	$_____	

5.	Gasoline	_____ estimated miles a year divided by miles per gallon of _____ times the average price of $_____ a gallon	$_____
6.	Oil changes	Cost of regular oil changes during the year	$_____
7.	Tires	Cost of tires purchased during the year	$_____
8.	Maintenance/repairs	Cost of planned or other expected maintenance	$_____
9.	Parking and tolls	Regular fees for parking and highway toll charges	$_____
	TOTAL VARIABLE COSTS	$_____	

TOTAL COSTS $_____

DIVIDED BY MILES FOR THE YEAR _____

EQUALS TOTAL COST PER MILE _____

(*) This estimate of vehicle depreciation is based on a *straight-line* approach—equal depreciation each year; a more realistic approach would be larger amounts in the early years of ownership, such as 25-30% the first year, 30-35% the second year; most cars lose 90 percent of their value by the time they are seven years old.

BUYING VS. LEASING AN AUTOMOBILE

- **Purpose** To compare costs associated with buying and leasing an automobile or other vehicle.
- **Instructions** Obtain costs related to leasing and buying a vehicle.

Section III Sheet C-8
Personal Finance
Second Ed., Kapoor,
Dlabay & Hughes
Pages 293-295

PURCHASE COSTS

- Total vehicle cost, including sales tax ($_____)

- Down payment (or full amount if paying cash) $_____

- Monthly loan payment $_____ times _____ month loan $_____
  (This item is zero if vehicle is not financed)

- Opportunity cost of down payment (or total cost of the vehicle if it is bought for cash)
  $_____ times ____ years of financing/ownership times ____ percent (interest rate which
  funds could earn) $_____

- Less: Estimated value of vehicle at end of loan term/ownership period $–_____

  TOTAL COST TO BUY $_____

LEASING COSTS

- Security deposit $_____

- Monthly lease payments: $_____ times ____ months $_____

- Opportunity cost of security deposit:
  $_____ times ____ year times ____ percent $_____

- End-of-lease charges (if applicable)(*) $_____

  TOTAL COST TO LEASE $_____

(*) With a closed-end lease, charges for extra mileage or excessive wear and tear; with an open-end lease, end-of-lease payment if appraised value is less than estimated ending value.

APARTMENT/HOME INSURANCE COMPARISON

- **Purpose** To research and compare companies, coverages, and costs for apartment or home insurance.
- **Instructions** Contact three insurance agents to obtain the information requested below.

Section III Sheet D-1
Personal Finance
Second Ed., Kapoor,
Dlabay & Hughes
Pages 338-343

Type of building: _____ apartment _____ home _____ condominium

Location _____

Type of construction _____ age of building _____

(If apartment or condominium, number of units in building? _____)

	Company A	Company B	Company C
Company name			
Insurance agent's name, address, and phone			
Coverage: Dwelling $_____ Other structures $_____ (garage, shed, etc.) (dwelling and other structure coverage does not apply to apartment/ condo insurance)	Premium	Premium	Premium
Personal property $_____			
Additional living expenses $_____			
Personal Liability Bodily injury $_____ Property damage $_____			
Medical payments per person $_____ per accident $_____			
Deductible amount			
Other coverage: _____ $_____			
Service charges or fees			
TOTAL PREMIUM			

AUTOMOBILE INSURANCE COST COMPARISON

Section III Sheet D-2
Personal Finance
Second Ed., Kapoor,
Dlabay & Hughes
Pages 343-351

- **Purpose** To research and compare companies, coverages, and costs for automobile insurance.
- **Instructions** Contact three insurance agents to obtain the information requested below.

Automobile (year, make, model, engine size) _____

Driver's age _____ Sex _____ Total miles driven a year _____

A.   Full-time or part-time driver? _____   Number of miles driven (one way) to work _____

B.   Driver's education completed? _____

C.   Accidents or traffic violations within the past three years? _____

	Company A	Company B	Company C
Company name			
Agent's name, address, phone			
Policy length (6 months, 1 year)			
Coverage: Bodily Injury Liability _____ per person _____ per accident	Premium	Premium	Premium
Property Damage Liability _____ per accident			
Collision _____ deductible			
Comprehensive _____ deductible			
Medical payments per person $_____			
Uninsured Motorists Liability per person $_____ per accident $_____			
Other coverage _____			
Service charges or fees			
TOTAL ANNUAL PREMIUM			

LIFE INSURANCE POLICY COMPARISON

- **Purpose** To research and compare companies, coverages, and costs for different life insurance policies.
- **Instructions** Analyze advertisements and contact life insurance agents to obtain the information requested below.

Section III Sheet D-3
Personal Finance
Second Ed., Kapoor,
Dlabay & Hughes
Pages 394-405

Age _____

	A	B	C
Company			
Agent's name, address, phone			
Type of insurance [term, straight/whole, limited payment (indicate number of years), endowment, universal]			
Type of policy (individual, group)			
Amount of coverage			
Frequency of payment (monthly, quarterly, semi-annual, annual)			
Premium amount			
Other costs: —service charge —physical exam			
Rate of return (annual percentage increase in cash value; not applicable for term policies)			
Benefits of insurance as stated in ad or by agent			
Potential problems or disadvantages of this coverage			

ASSESSING RISK FOR INVESTMENTS

- **Purpose** To assess the risk of various investments in relation to your personal risk tolerance and financial goals.
- **Instructions** List various investments you are considering based on the type and level of risk associated with each.

Section III Sheet E-1
Personal Finance
Second Ed., Kapoor,
Dlabay & Hughes
Pages 426-430

Type of risk	Loss of value (market risk)	Inflation risk	Interest rate risk	Liquidity risk
Level of risk				
High risk				
Moderate risk				
Low risk				
No risk				

INVESTMENT BROKER COMPARISON

Section III Sheet E-2
Personal Finance
Second Ed., Kapoor,
Dlabay & Hughes
Pages 468-470

- **Purpose** To compare the benefits and costs of different investment brokers.
- **Instructions** When considering using the services of an investment broker, compare factors listed below.

Broker's name		
Organization		
Address		
Phone		
Years of experience		
Education and other training		
Areas of specialization		
Certifications held		
Professional affiliations		
Employer's stock exchange and financial market affiliations		
Information services offered		
Minimum commission charge		
Commission on 100 shares of stock at $50/share		
Fees for other investments: • corporate bonds • mutual funds • stock options		
Other fees: • annual account fee • inactivity fee • other _____		

I.R.A. COMPARISON

- **Purpose** To compare the benefits and costs associated with different types and sources of individual retirement accounts.
- **Instructions** Analyze advertisements and articles, and contact various financial institutions to obtain the information requested below.

Section III Sheet F-1
Personal Finance
Second Ed., Kapoor,
Dlabay & Hughes
Pages 586-588

	Bank or Savings and Loan	Mutual Fund or Stock Broker	Credit Union or Life Insurance Co.
Name of Financial Institution			
Address			
Type of account of type of investments (savings certificate, stocks, bonds)			
Minimum initial deposit			
Minimum additional deposits			
Current rate of return			
Service charges/fees			
Safety: Insured? By who? Amount			
Payroll deduction available			
Special offers: —"free" gifts —"bonus" interest			
Penalty for early withdrawal: a. IRS penalty (10%) b. other penalty			
Other features or restrictions			
SAMPLE ACCOUNT GROWTH: Starting at age _____, depositing $2,000 a year, for _____ years will grow to $_____.			

RETIREMENT HOUSING & LIFE SITUATION PLANNING

- **Purpose** To consider housing alternatives for retirement living, and to plan retirement pursuits.
- **Instructions** Evaluate current and expected needs and interests based on the items below.

Section III Sheet F-2
Personal Finance
Second Ed., Kapoor,
Dlabay & Hughes
Pages 574-576

Retirement housing plans:

Description of current housing situation (size, facilities, location) _____

_____

_____

Time until retirement _____ years

Description of retirement housing needs _____

_____

Checklist of retirement housing alternatives:

____ present home
____ housesharing
____ accessory apartment
____ elder cottage housing
____ rooming house
____ single-room occupancy
____ caretaker arrangement

____ professional companionship arrangement
____ commercial rental
____ board and care home
____ congregate housing
____ continuing care retirement community
____ nursing home

Personal and financial factors that will influence the retirement housing decision _____

_____

Financial planning actions to be taken related to retirement housing _____

_____

Retirement activities:

1. What plans do you have to work part time or do volunteer work? _____

    _____

2. What recreational activities do you plan to continue or start? _____

    _____

    Location, training, equipment needs _____

    _____

3. What plans do you have for travel or educational study? _____

    _____

    Information needed, contacts _____

    _____